Forex Trading

Intermediate Strategies

By

John Gibson

Copyright 2018 by John Gibson - All rights reserved.

The following book is reproduced below with the goal of providing information that is as accurate and reliable as possible. Regardless, purchasing this book can be seen as consent to the fact that both the publisher and the author of this book are in no way experts on the topics discussed within and that any recommendations or suggestions that are made herein are for entertainment purposes only. Professionals should be consulted as needed prior to undertaking any of the action endorsed herein.

This declaration is deemed fair and valid by both the American Bar Association and the Committee of Publishers Association and is legally binding throughout the United States.

Furthermore, the transmission, duplication or reproduction of any of the following work including specific information will be considered an illegal act irrespective of if it is done electronically or in print. This extends to creating a secondary or tertiary copy of the work or a recorded copy and is only allowed with express written consent from the Publisher. All additional right reserved.

The information in the following pages is broadly considered to be a truthful and accurate account of facts and as such any inattention, use or misuse of the information in question by the reader will render any resulting actions solely under their purview. There are no scenarios in which the publisher or the original author of this work can be in any fashion deemed liable for any hardship or damages that may befall them after undertaking information described herein.

Additionally, the information in the following pages is intended only for informational purposes and should thus be thought of as universal. As befitting its nature, it is presented without assurance regarding its prolonged validity or interim quality. Trademarks that are mentioned are done without written consent and can in no way be considered an endorsement from the trademark holder.

Table of Contents

Introduction 4

Chapter 1: The T/R Axis- Unlocking Trends 7

Chapter 2: Turning Points and PA Relevance 19

Chapter 3: Support and Resistance Rediscovered 31

Chapter 4: Timeframe Mechanics 49

Chapter 5: The Complete System- A Live Trade 69

Introduction

Thank you for buying this book. Mastering the forex markets is no easy task. The forex markets are dynamic and constantly changing in character. A successful forex trader has to marshal all their available mental and technical resources and be able to deploy it in real time at a moment's notice. Such an ability requires countless hours of training and the ability to pick oneself up after repeated failures. It requires us to re-define their assumptions of success and failure. It requires us to examine ourselves with a microscope and not flinch when we find something painful. In short, it requires us to do things which do not come to human beings naturally.

The good news is that trading successfully is a process. Processes involve a number of clearly defined, executable steps which deliver an intended result. Learning such a process is a difficult but perfectly achievable task. This series of books will walk you through this process while helping guide you on how to implement the habits you need to trade successfully. Some of you may have read the first book in this series. For those of you who have, this is a step further in your journey to trading forex successfully. Those of you picking up this book without reading its predecessor, fret not. The concepts in this book are similar to those previously explained but do understand, I will be assuming a certain level of understanding of the markets and its terms within you.

In the first book, I introduced you to the trend strength analysis method and how to use it as a bedrock of your trading analysis routine. Here, I will take you on a deeper dive of the basics and examine it further, especially the interaction between the elements of trend strength with support and resistance. These concepts build on what was previously explained and will enhance your understanding and, I hope, appreciation for the complex, chaotic beast that is the market. The chapters in this book are extremely dense and contain a lot of information so do take your time with it. Lots of practice is necessary before you can trade this system successfully and those of you expecting a plug and play system will be disappointed. I laid out a few plug and play systems in the previous book which rely only on a cursory understanding of trend strength so there's always that option. However, the concepts explained here will deepen your understanding to the extent that you will never need indicators or patterns anymore. You will be able to trade by simply looking at a price chart.

If that seems like an impossible reality then, read on. This book will fully flesh out the technical side of trading before future books in the series address the topics of mindset and risk management which are just as important. Study the charts in here carefully and practice deliberately and with patience and I promise you, you will be in possession of a trading method which will stand the test of time.

Good luck on your journey!

Chapter 1: The T/R Axis- Unlocking Trends

The price of any instrument on a chart is constantly fluctuating between two states of existence, namely, a trending state and a ranging state. A trend is simply a state where price has a direction, either up or down. It doesn't matter how rapidly it is progressing in a given direction, as long as it has one, the market is considered to be trending. A ranging market or a market in a range is one which has no direction, that is, it is moving sideways. It is essential to think of the market direction as being somewhere on an axis we will refer to as the "Trend/Range" axis or T/R axis for short.

An instrument which is moving rapidly in a given direction, where all the price bars or candles within it are only those with trend, that is, if the market is moving upwards and all the candles are bullish or the market is moving downwards and all the candles are bearish, is an example of an extreme in the T/R axis. Such a market would sit firmly on the Trend (T) side of the axis. Similarly, a market which is moving sideways perfectly within a range, with the top and bottom almost perfectly aligning themselves, will be considered to be on the range (R) side of the axis.

The T/R axis forms the basis of our understanding of how markets work and what the price and order flow mechanics are beneath the charts. Understanding the order flow of an instrument is the surest way of trading it successfully as opposed to using an indicator which is derived from the price. Think about it, which scenario would be easier to interpret? If someone were to tell you exactly who was buying and selling at a given moment, how much they were buying and selling and at what levels they were doing so, would you have any difficulty in forming a picture of the market? You probably would not. Would giving you an indicator derived on a mathematical interpretation of price bring you closer than this to forming a picture of the market? The answer is clear. Order flow is the surest way to decipher market mechanics and remains the only infallible way to trade successfully. The order flow can be interpreted in many ways but using the price mechanics and price action to do so is the easiest since price is the first reflection of the underlying order flow. Using an indicator derived from price puts us 2 levels further away from the order flow.

The T/R axis location of a given instrument at a given moment helps us to identify certain important information about that instrument, namely:

- The distribution of order flow between with trend (WT) and counter trend (CT) players at that moment.
- The direction in which the market is headed, if there is one.

While the direction can be figured out visually, the order flow distribution is a bit trickier. It has visual elements to it and, indeed, after regular practice you will be able to do so at a glance, but when starting out with this method, the T/R axis helps simplify this. This is because the T/R axis works on a simple principle: the greater the number of CT players in the market, the further towards the R side of the axis is the market. The lesser the number of CT players, the more towards the T side of the axis is the market. Visually, the charts on the next few pages illustrate this statement.

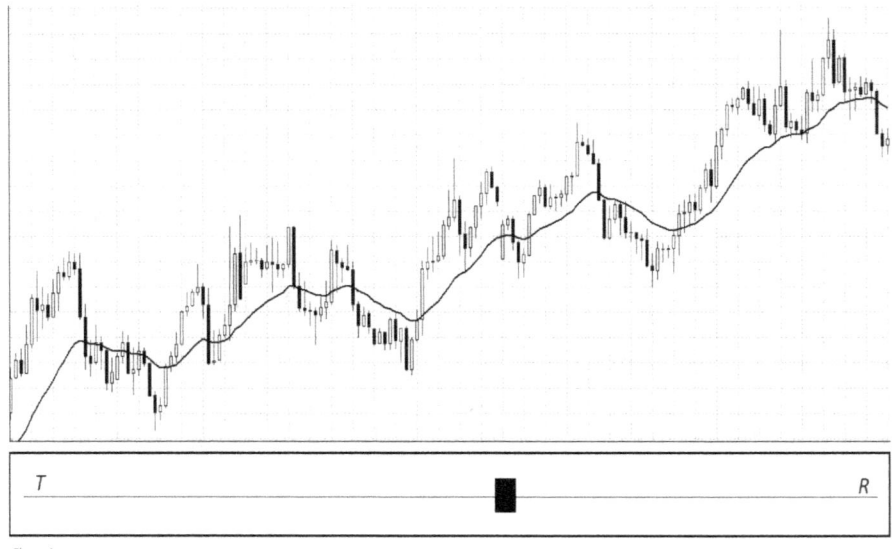

Figure 1

In Figure 1 above, we see an uptrend (looking left to right price is headed upwards) but clearly there are CT players present. Remember, the greater the number of counter trend players present, the more to the right our place on the T/R axis shifts. Here, we can see our chart sits on the right half of the axis (denoted by the black solid rectangle on the T/R axis below the chart) since the number of CT players is significant. This chart doesn't sit all the way to the right since the WT players are still able to push price upwards despite CT presence. Don't get hung up on exactly where I've placed the chart on the T/R axis. What is important is that you roughly understand where it lies. For example, if you placed it a few centimeters to the left, it isn't incorrect. Placing it closer to the T side though, would be incorrect. The idea is to get a gist of what's going on.

It is important when analyzing a trend that we take into account a substantial portion of it as well as place more emphasis on the more recent price action. This is something that is very subjective of course and depends a lot on your own preferred "zoom" level on the markets. When I say recent price action, I do not mean the last few bars but more like the current stage plus the previous rise and previous consolidation at the very least. In Figure 1 previously as we saw, I've placed the chart slightly to the right of the midpoint of the T/R axis. If I were to take into full account the price action from the left of that chart, I might have placed it further to the right on the T/R scale. The reason it sits more to the left in this case is I'm giving the more recent price action greater weight starting from the midpoint of that chart. I'm quite comfortable doing this because I've found from experience that this view gives me the most comfort and clearest picture on the market. You must endeavor to find your own custom "zoom" level on the markets through practice.

Here are some tips and indicators with regards to evaluating a chart on the T/R axis:

- Look at the number of CT bars versus WT bars. Specific properties to look for include:
    - The number of each. There's no need to count them individually, just get an idea of the distribution.
    - The size of the CT bars compared to the WT bars. How much of distance covered by the WT bars is taken out by the CT bars for example.
- Evaluate the CT bars themselves:
    - Are the CT candles bodies big and do they close near the highs/lows? Or do they have wicks and tails? A stronger candle means greater force behind the move.
    - What are the recent CT candles like compared to the ones in the past? Are they getting bigger? Smaller? More in number? Less in number? Same in number but less forceful? And so on.

- Also evaluate the WT bars, specifically:

    - What are the recent WT bars like compared to the ones in the past? Smaller, bigger, more in number, less in number etc.

This is not an exhaustive list and neither is it a checklist. When starting out do use it as one but as you become more familiar with this skill, you will begin to form a mental picture without the need to quantify anything. Let us walk through this list using the chart in Figure 1 previously shown.

As the chart stands currently, we can see that the number of CT bars has become progressively lesser than in the past. This does not mean they've disappeared but their frequency has reduced. The bar size of the CT bars remains in about the same proportion to the WT as in the past. The CT bars are maintaining the same size pretty much with most of them being big bodied and strong. What has really changed is the frequency of the CT and WT bars. To the left we can see every single push upwards was met with an immediate reaction from the CT players. As we move to the right, we can see the frequency of the CT bars decrease and the frequency of the

WT bars increase. This explains how price has been able to make new highs despite seemingly decent CT presence. (An easy visual way to decipher this is to look at simply the color of the bars in the left half versus the right half of the chart). As things stand we can come to the conclusion that the chart is moving steadily to the left on the T/R axis as it progresses. This may change of course, it may start moving to the right before moving to the left. Or it might abruptly charge towards the right. We must recognize that such things happen and that there are no definitive answers in the market. We simply recognize that the odds of the chart continuing to trend with its position moving to the left on the T/R axis is good. Let's take a look at a few more examples.

Figure 2

Figure 2 illustrates a chart where the price action lies firmly on the right side of the T/R axis. I usually designate a range as such when there's 2 hits to the top and the bottom. The lack of 2 hits on the bottom is the only thing preventing this chart from being all the way on the right of the T/R axis. As we work our way from the left of the chart notice how the bullish pushbacks build steadily and increase in number. Both in terms of the size of the bullish (CT) bars as well as the length of the overall pushbacks, the bullish presence increases. Finally we see the bear trend descend into a small range where no further lows are made before the bulls push back rapidly towards a prior swing high. There is no bearish presence whatsoever on this push upwards as we can see no bearish candles formed. This is very significant given that we've just experienced a strong bear trend. Price pushes past the prior swing high a bit before forming a wick and consolidating at the level.

Here we can see the most recent price action has strong bullish presence. However, when evaluating the placement on the T/R axis, it is important to take a bigger picture as mentioned in the prior example. For this particular example,

I'm considering all the price action from the middle of the chart onwards with a little weight given to what happened on the left. This "zoom" level is a bit different from the previous chart where I took a greater portion of the price action on the left into account and I'm sure this is a sticking point for you. After all, how does one determine an ideal zoom level when it keeps changing depending on the chart?

This is a question that I will answer in the chapter on turning points. For now, concentrate only on observing the nature of WT and CT price action using the checklist previously mentioned. You need to train your mind to think this way and the only way to do so is to look at as many charts as possible and see how much of the characteristics mentioned you can spot. Another piece of advice I often give is to think of the market as a river flowing in a direction. How many obstacles are present in its path? Are the obstacles increasing in number? Have they increased to such an extent that the direction of flow might reverse all together? In figure 2 this certainly seems to be the case. The market was "flowing" downwards and the obstacles kept pushing back little by little until they stalled the downward flow all together. They finally pushed back strongly in the opposite direction and the original direction of the flow seems to be reversing.

For those of you who have read the first book, the position of the chart on the T/R axis is an indication of trend strength. The more to the right the chart is on the T/R axis, the weaker the trend strength is. The more on the left, the stronger it is. The more to the right of the T/R axis we move, the greater is the presence of the CT players and thus weaker the WT players. This is why the trend strength is low. While the strategies given in the first book required you to only have a cursory understanding of trend strength and turning points, in this book, it is imperative that you gain a deeper understanding of this concept.

A point of confusion I often observe amongst those studying this: People often mistake the T/R axis to be an approximation of trend direction. This is not the case! It is easy to be misled into thinking that the left of the axis represents a downtrend and the right an uptrend but as you can see from examples above, the placement on the left or right of the T/R axis has nothing to do with trend direction. So guard yourself from making this error.

Another sticking point is the level of "zoom" you need or in other words, how much price action is relevant to our consideration for placement on the T/R axis. This will be addressed now in the next chapter by understanding the concept of turning points.

Chapter 2: Turning Points and PA Relevance

A basic rule or piece of wisdom everyone agrees on with regards to trading is to trade with the trend as much and as often as possible. What is more difficult is to determine what the direction of the trend is at a given moment. Visually, a lot of charts may be going, say, upwards when looking left to right but if the chart sits on the extreme right of the T/R axis, indicating a very strong or equal counter trend presence, then the simple visual way becomes suspect. Another sticking point as we saw in the previous chapter is that determining the appropriate amount of price action to take into account is subjective or to be more accurate, thus far appears to be subjective.

Both these issues are solved by understanding the concept of turning points. Essentially, turning points are zones or swing points above or below which we switch our bias to the other side of the market. A turning point is a Rubicon of sorts on the charts where the WT players mark a line in the sand and do their absolute best to defend it with the knowledge that, should this level fall to the CT players, the best thing to so would be to join the other side of the market. From an order flow perspective let us dig deeper into why turning points behave the way they do. As price moves in a given direction in a trend the CT players constantly try to pushback into it. Their efforts are overcome by the WT players and the trend continues. No trend lasts forever though and as the Wt players lose steam, the CT players increase in strength. This strength is further increased by those traders who do not have a stake on either side of the market, and noting the increased CT strength, choose to join that side.

Eventually the CT players mount a serious challenge which requires a huge effort from the WT players to overcome. This often prints as a volatile range or a swing point with a good to massive WT reaction. This level is where the WT players overcame the strongest challenge to the CT players. The CT strength though is only increasing. As price moves, with trend, past the level where the WT players overcame the CT forces, the CT players regroup to attack and push price to the same level again. On the charts, this will look like a push back or a swing back to the earlier swing point or range which was defended by the WT players. As traders we can safely reach a conclusion that this level which is currently under attack is an important one since this was where the WT players overcame the strongest CT challenge yet. It stands to reason the same traders who defended this level will defend it again with the same enthusiasm. If this level were to fall, the strongest of the WT force will be spent and the CT players would have no opposition. In other words, this level is a line in the sand for the WT players. If price goes beyond this level CT, any WT traders holding their positions will face a serious loss and will certainly liquidate their positions. In effect, such a liquidation will turn the previous CT players into the new WT side because they will be the dominant force in the market and hence, will dictate the dominant trend.

Such a level then is a turning point on the charts. On either side of this level lie the CT and WT players ready to defend their sides of the market. Any strong close on either side of this level determines whether we, as traders, keep our existing trend bias or flip our bias to the other side. In terms of the T/R axis, as a trend begins, we will often find ourselves on the left of the axis since CT presence will be low. As the trend progresses and CT presence increases, we steadily move to the right. Eventually we find ourselves on or near the extreme right as the CT and WT presence is roughly equal and that price has reached a turning point. In this way, the T/R axis helps us identify a turning point on the charts but I wouldn't use it as a primary tool to identify such a level. Instead, the key characteristics to look for are:

- A volatile range where CT presence is high and there are repeated attacks on the top of the range. Only strong WT presence helps force price in the WT direction. Such a range will usually have a CT tilt to it.

- A swing high or low depending on whether the trend is bearish or bullish respectively. The high or low of this swing is where the WT players come in and reject the CT forces. Such a swing point will have a massive or at the very least, strong WT push upwards. It will also have a strong CT push into it.

Understanding the order flow specifics that lead to the formation of these levels is crucial. Resist the temptation to apply the above two bullet points in a rote fashion and instead think in terms of "Where on this chart have the CT players mounted their strongest opposition yet? Where have the WT players had to expend the most energy to overcome that opposition?" Once you think in these terms it should be obvious why a turning point usually presents itself as either a volatile range or a swing point with a good reaction. In addition, the T/R axis gives us advance warning as to whether we ought to be on the lookout for the trend flipping or not.

Again, if we understand the order flow, this should be clear. As a trend progresses, the greater the CT presence. Greater the CT presence, greater the odds of the trend flipping. Also, greater the CT presence, the more to the right we travel on the T/R axis. Hence, the further to the right we travel, the more likely it is that a trend reversal is imminent. Now, this is not always the case since the markets are chaotic and resist any sort of fixed definition imposed on them. It is however largely true. Encountering the odd volatile range which results in a further strong trend continuation with price never coming back to it doesn't invalidate the principle.

To address the problem of how much price action to consider before fixing a spot on the T/R axis, see whether price is past or within the turning point in the direction of the trend. That is, in a bearish trend is it below the turning point? Or in a bullish trend is it above it? If the turning point still hasn't been breached, then we need to consider the entirety of the trend's price action with more weight being given to the recent price action and decreasing as we go progressively to the left of the price chart, as described in the previous chapter. If the turning point has been breached, then we only consider the price action which as led up to the breach. More often than not, the push through the level will be strong and we will find ourselves all the way on the left of the T/R axis again. This stands to reason since a new trend has formed.

The T/R axis also functions as a guard against false breakouts, the bane of any trend following trader. If we are approaching the top or bottom of a previous volatile range we've designated as a turning point and we want to make sure that a break of this level will result in price following through and not whipsawing back, then take a look at your T/R axis position. Ideally we ought to be somewhere close to extreme right. If we're still near the middle or a bit past it, then the odds are good that a false breakout is about to occur. The reasoning is simple. If the T/R position isn't all the way to the right, this indicates that we don't think the CT presence is high enough. A false breakout is essentially the result of a weak CT presence losing steam fast in the presence of dominant WT players. Thus, the T/R positioning alerts us in advance of what might possibly happen. Again, not all false breakouts can be avoided because trading is not an endeavor where we seek to hit a 100% on everything. My book on risk management and mindset address this in greater detail.

These 2 concepts, the T/R axis and turning points go a long way towards demystifying trends and their direction. I haven't addressed entering a position as yet because it is useless to do so unless you grasp these basic points. My advise is to open up your charts and practice this until it becomes second nature for you to spot the location of the T/R axis and the relevant turning point and whether price has breached it or not. The charts in the next few pages illustrate how to think in this manner.

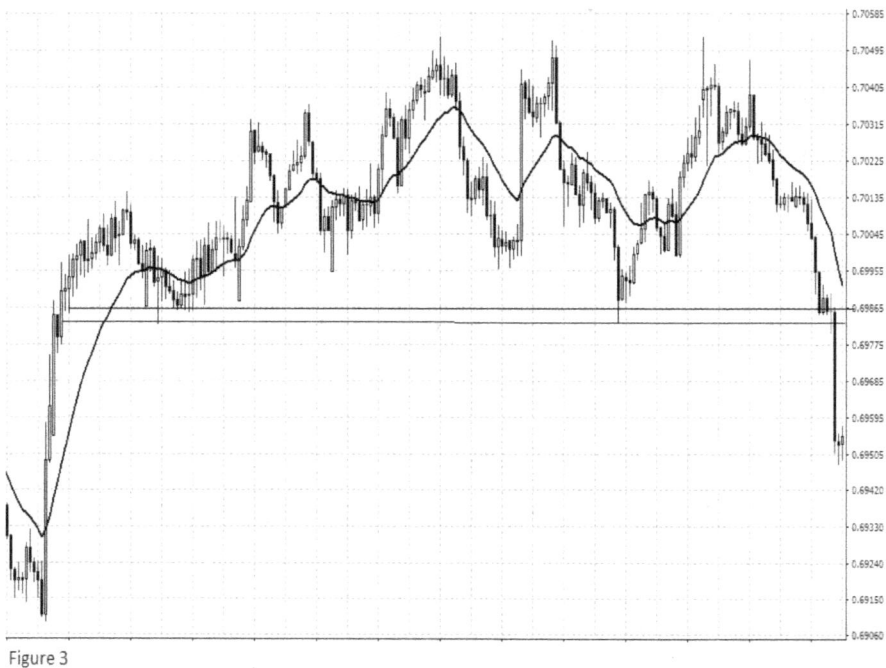
Figure 3

Figure 3 shows a bull trend culminating in a very volatile range. This is a static chart but imagine watching the price action as it progresses from left to right. We will steadily see an increase in bearish presence and our position on the T/R axis will slide continuously to the right. Once we reach all the way to the right and price breaches the turning point on this timeframe, we can conclude that the trend is now bearish and our position on the T/R axis is all the way to the left given the almost non existent bullish presence.

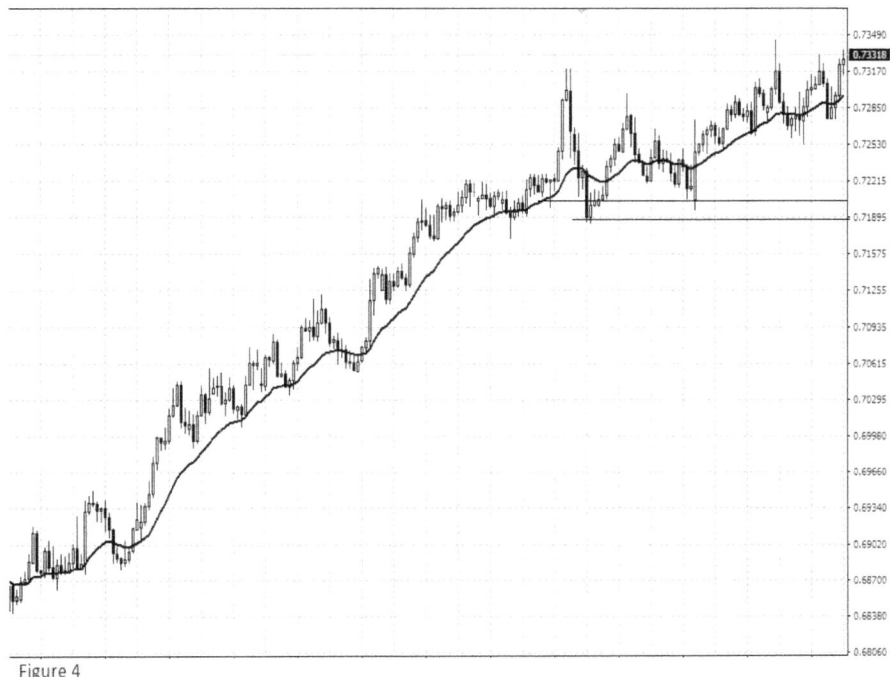

Figure 4

How do we determine a turning point as a trend progresses? At the current position of price on this chart, we see one clear spot where the bears tried imposing control only for the bulls to reject them swiftly, though not with the same force. Note the bearish pressure into the swing point, the immediate bullish reaction which creates a "V" shape reversal and how the retest of the swing point failed to reach it and was instead rejected by a big bullish bar. Cover this chart with a piece of paper and uncover the chart moving left to right. Practice designating turning points as the trend progresses.

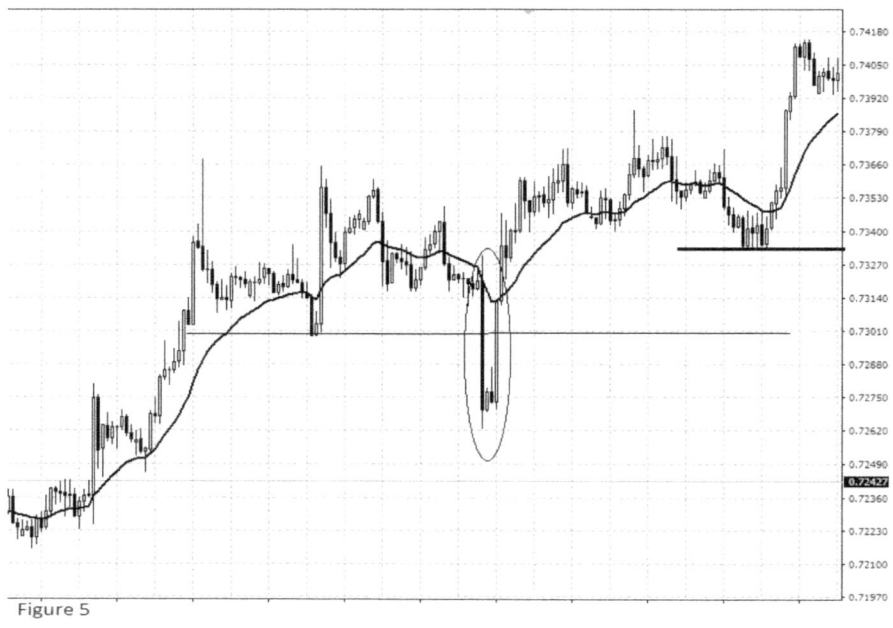
Figure 5

The T/R axis can guard against false breakouts as we see here in figure 5. The false breakout is marked with a circle. At first glance this seems legit given the size of the bearish bar. However, ask yourself where on the T/R axis would we have been prior to this bar? What is the size of the previous bearish bars compared to this one? The frequency compared to the bullish bars? Notice how prior to this bar, a number of bearish bars in the sideways correction struggle to undo the move of a single bullish bar. This would lead us to place ourselves somewhere just past the center on the T/R axis. So despite a break of the turning point (the thin horizontal line), we would have been alert to this possibility. Price subsequently moves on and the latest turning point is marked with a thick horizontal line. Can you see why?

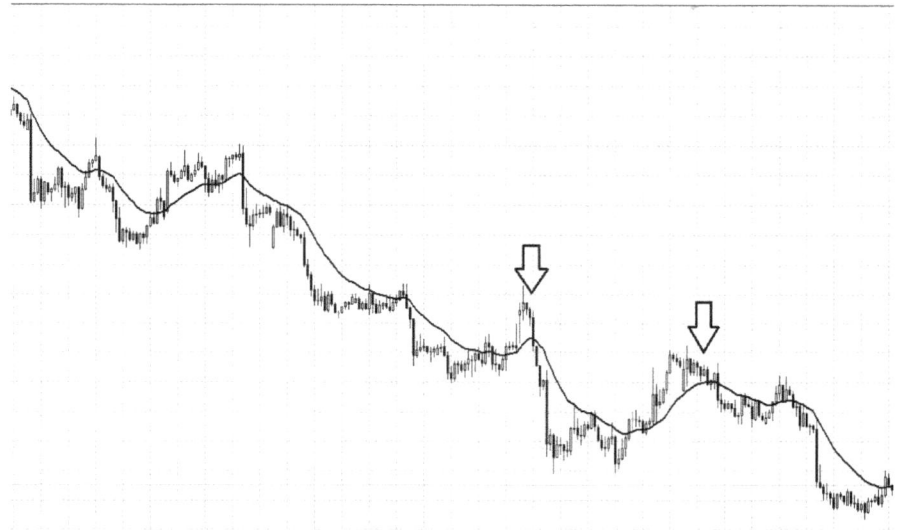

Figure 6

Remember to look at and understand the order flow characteristics of what makes turning points powerful. Here we see two relevant swing highs in downtrend in figure 6. Which would you designate as the turning point. Taking into account the reaction from the top of the swing high and the swiftness with which price was rejected, the swing on the left is more appropriate. The one on the right shows only a moderate rejection even though it gained steam later. The key is to understand WT presence at the level itself so we can approximate how it'll be defended when price comes back to it, if it ever does. Looking at the 2 reactions from the respective levels, where do you think the greater bearish presence is? Where is it stronger? Consequently, which is more likely to hold off a bullish attack?

This concludes for now our look at turning points and indeed the characteristics of trend identification. Readers of the previous book in the series will appreciate at how much deeper an understanding there is to be gained of the markets using the trend strength approach and in using turning points to determine which direction the market is headed in. It was at this point in the previous book, we started looking at strategies using indicators. Indeed, for a beginner who wants to get their feet wet in the markets, this would be the appropriate jump off point.

To really understand the market and gain an even greater edge though, we need to next look at something which has always been explained in other books but never really understood properly in relation to trends: Support and Resistance.

Chapter 3: Support and Resistance Rediscovered

Any beginner strategy which implements price action takes into account support and resistance levels. There is however a misunderstanding of what support and resistance actually is and what constitutes a level. Most advice is some variation of "look at the reactions off the level" or "look at the number of hits on it" etc. This is technically correct but there is something implied in those statements which is not true. If we only consider levels which have strong reaction off of them to be proper S/R levels, the implication is the levels which do not have strong reactions are not good levels. Such a conclusion will cause us to miss out on many good trade opportunities.

Another mistake that struggling traders often make is to give S/R primary importance in their trading strategies. This is an offshoot of the previously mentioned wrong implication. Basing your entire strategy only around S/R levels is better, of course, than relying on an indicator which is two or three levels removed from price. It does, however, cause us to completely ignore the price action itself. Think about it. A price action strategy that doesn't incorporate any price action mechanics into it! What is needed is to go back to the basics of S/R and understand what it is and understand it from an order flow perspective.

As buyers and sellers interact in the market and as the price flows towards some direction (sideways included), the volume with which the opposing market forces collide leaves tell tale signs. Such a collision often prints as a rejection of a level or a reversal or direction. The location of this collision is often remembered by those who partook in it and by those who understand order flow mechanics. Therefore when price re-approaches this collision point, the traders who previously defended or broke through that particular location, take part once more and it becomes a gathering point of sorts for both sides of the market to express their views on how price ought to go next. This collision or gathering point is what a support level or a resistance level essentially is. It is not a pretty trend line that price hugs just because the line exists or it is not some range bottom that price repeatedly bounces off because the line is perfectly horizontal. The S/R level is created because of order flow NOT because of the fact that you can draw a pretty line through it which is ram rod straight.

Now, here's something crucial to recognize. Buyers and sellers exist all over the charting landscape. Its just that in certain locations they exist in greater number than others. What this means is that every single point on the chart which has had any interaction between a buyer and a seller which resulted in some reaction or rejection of that level is a potential S/R point. Take some time to understand that sentence again. What I'm saying is every single location where price has been rejected, no matter how minuscule the rejection, is an S/R level. This is in complete opposition to how S/R is usually thought about. To make it even more clear what I mean: A minor or major or key S/R level is not determined just by the size of the reaction off it. You could have a level which has seen a big reaction off it in the past but, using principles I will explain shortly, I may still be inclined to designate that level as a minor one and one that is unimportant.

So how does one determine which level is a major one or a minor one? The answer is that determining the strength of a given level is a combination of two things which need to be evaluated simultaneously:

- The strength of the rejections or hits on that level.

- The trend strength headed into that level. In other words, where on the T/R axis does our current price action lie?

The best way to explain this concept is by using an example. Lets say there's a vehicle which is traveling along a highway. This vehicle is subjected to two forces at all times, as are all vehicles on the road, the forces of acceleration (WT forces) and braking/friction (CT forces). The proportion in which these two forces exist determines the overall speed of the vehicle (the trend strength or position on the T/R axis). Higher the acceleration (WT) and lower the braking (CT), the higher the speed is. Similarly, lower the acceleration (WT) and higher the braking (CT), lower the speed. If no acceleration is applied to the vehicle it will eventually come to a stop due to the frictional forces acting on it.

Now let's imagine there an obstacle in front of this vehicle on the highway. Now this obstacle has some potential to stop this vehicle (the number of CT players ready to oppose the WT forces). If however, the speed with which the vehicle approaches the obstacle is extremely high, it will most likely blow through this it. Sure there might be some retardation of speed depending on how big the obstacle is but a high speed will result in larger momentum which will overpower whatever potential the obstacle has to oppose said momentum.

There will also be a limit beyond which the speed of the vehicle will not make any difference in determining whether or not it gets past the obstacle. In other words, if the obstacle is the size of mount Everest, it does not matter how fast the vehicle approaches it, there's no way it is going to get through. Hence, determining whether our vehicle overcomes the obstacle or not depends on the speed with which it is approaching the obstacle and the size of the obstacle itself.

Similarly, determining whether an S/R level will hold in the face of an attack from price depends on the strength with which price approaches it and the strength of the level itself. There will always be levels which are simply too strong to overcome and price will be rejected from them no matter how strongly it approaches it. Going back to our example, the vehicle might hit the obstacle, bounce backwards, gather more energy and hit the obstacle again and again until it finally breaks through. We see examples of this behavior over and over again in the markets. Another observation we can make while thinking like this is: when price is moving with great strength in a trend, it requires very little coaxing to continue to do so. In other words, when trend strength is high (and any pullbacks/CT presence are small as a consequence), price requires very little encouragement to stop pulling back and to continue on its original direction. Even a small push will be enough to stop the pullback/CT action and resume the trend. Therefore, any level where even a small number of WT players and CT players interacted previously is a good enough gathering point for WT players to resume the trend and end the CT reaction due to the sheer size and strength of the WT contingent.

I appreciate this sort of thinking is not common amongst readily available trading sources who preach and teach price action. To explain what I'm saying in another way: It is the trend strength which guides us as to which S/R levels to pay attention to except in cases when the S/R level is extremely strong. So as you can see now, evaluating a chart by starting with the S/R levels is doing things the wrong way around. It is the T/R axis position which should be evaluated first and only then based on that do we move on to see which S/R levels can perpetuate the trend or hold off an attack on them from the trend. The S/R levels are also where we can finally address something I deliberately haven't touched upon so far. Our trade entry locations.

The S/R levels is where we enter our positions in the direction of the prevalent trend. When price reacts into these levels, we base our entry decision on the basis of the position of the T/R axis and the relative strength of the level. Again, I understand that this is an almost alien way of trading because conventional advice with regards to entry decisions is to look for multiple confirmations between indicators and to wait for a formation of some sort. What you need to understand is this: Those confirmations and patterns are a direct result of order flow. Order flow and price mechanics are what dictate the patterns you see on the chart, not the other way around. If you can read the order flow, then why would you need any confirmation. You can effectively see where buyers and sellers are parked and in what strength so why would you need to wait from some formation or candlestick pattern to form to "confirm" what you're seeing? The T/R axis and relative S/R strength to the T/R axis offer all the confirmation you need!

The major challenge in trading this way is the mental execution. Some traders will feel naked trading this way since all you need is a price chart. It also goes against popular mainstream advice which has unfortunately conditioned traders into believing that the market needs to give them some sort of secret signal to coax them into opening a position. Never mind that this secret signal is known by everyone and his mother and that entire hordes of such traders are sitting everywhere looking for the same thing. A basic rule of economics is that of supply and demand. When one rises the other falls. Similarly, the more the number of traders looking at the same indicator, the less is its effectiveness. This is why many indicators used the old fashioned way such as the MACD etc do not work anymore. This is why you cannot make money using a simple EMA crossover strategy. You need to understand order flow and trend strength. In my previous book, I outlined strategies that use these indicators but even then I added a layer of trend strength to enhance their effectiveness.

Trend strength as an approach is evergreen because it results in deciphering order flow directly. It is not deriving anything or building complicated mathematical formulas over existing indicators. Our quest as traders should not be to complicate things. Instead we should dig deeper into the fundamentals. This is what the trend strength approach allows you to do. If you still feel uncomfortable placing so called naked entries like this, feel free to use the strategies in my previous book. Understand though that you're still using the same technique but deliberately placing a layer between the market and yourself because of your mental discomfort. Your job is to understand and eliminate that discomfort, not to seek a better or palatable strategy.

Now that I've completed that little digression, lets get back to understanding S/R and trade entries better. If I had to sum up this approach as a rule of thumb it would be this: when trend strength is high (T/R axis on the left extreme or close to it), almost any minor level which as had a reaction will be enough to perpetuate the trend. So when price pulls back into it weakly (as it does when trend strength is high), the odds are good that the level will be able to hold the pullback and resume the trend. Conversely, as our position on the T/R axis move to the right, the stronger our levels need to be. When price pulls back into the trend, we need to locate levels which are stronger and further inside the trend since the CT presence is high (as indicated by the T/R axis) to enter in direction of the trend.

I'm a huge advocate of only trading with the trend but there are traders who prefer counter trend trading. My advice to them is to do so when the T/R position is to the right. This means the CT presence is high and chances are your counter trend trades will have more time and force behind them to come to fruition. In a sideways movement, that is if the T/R is on the extreme right, we can trade both sides of the range irrespective of the trend since, by the position of the T/R, there is no trend. Hence, both sides of the market are valid. The following charts will help visualize what's been said better. As always, make sure to practice extensively on your own.

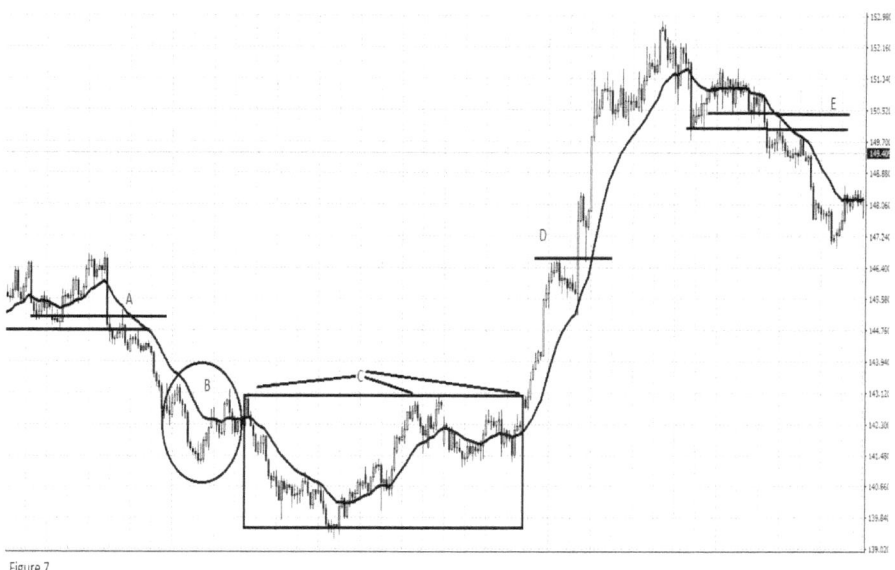

Figure 7

Figure 7 illustrates how S/R relevance changes as trend strength changes. Starting from the left, we can see a strong bear trend emerge with a huge bearish bar following weak buying compared to previous selling (note how many bullish bars it takes to undo the previous selling effort). Our position on the T/R axis is to the left. Therefore once price breaks through the S/R level A (which is a zone, as are all S/R levels), we can safely assume that A will behave as a good resistance given the current trend strength. Price tests the level and forms a pin bar and drops precipitously. Our next area of interest is within the circle marked by "B". In here we can see that after the downswing, buying interest ramps up and thus our T/R position moves more to the right. This means we need to seek appropriately strong S/R levels for trend continuation. The previous swing high seems a logical point given the force of the downswing from it (as opposed to the swing low just before it. Note the relative strengths of those 2 levels. The reaction off the swing low is minuscule and there's no way that level will hold price while it approaches with current trend strength).

Price halts just before B, forms yet another pin, and drops after a brief retest. We ought to be on the alert now though since we have seen, post the circle B, how buying strength is increasing. After price makes a new low (within the box C), we see buyers push price all the way back up. Given this level of buying interest, we need an even stronger S/R level and what better than the level we previously sold from? (B within the circle). This also happens to be our turning point so if this level folds we can safely assume the trend has flipped to bullish. Price approaches it with extreme bullishness and conservative trades would be justified in sitting out this retest of this level. Price reacts briefly downwards but then retests it again weakly. Since we now have evidence that there are some bears willing to defend this level, we join in and price duly drifts downwards.

It forms a higher low in a further indication that the trend is flipping. It moves towards the same level again (top of the rectangular box C). We would be justified in selling this level again given the previous reactions off it. Price however bulldozes through with huge bullish strength. This being our turning point, we can safely assume the trend has flipped to bullish. As an aside, take a moment to visually extrapolate the S/R line at A all the way to where price is now post this break of the box C. Conventional wisdom would have you selling A again because of the strong prior reactions from it. Look, however, at the massive strength with which price is approaching it. Our T/R position is firmly on the left and we will need an extremely strong level to be able to stop this freight train. Price reacts at D and then takes off again past it. Notice the pin bar testing D from above and then shooting upwards. This is because the bullish strength is such that even a minor level D, which barely elicited a bearish reaction, can function as an important S/R level. If we only entered trades at conventionally strong S/R levels without paying attention to the T/R positioning, we would have missed out on this profitable trade.

Turn your attention next to the level marked "E". Evaluate this the same way we've just looked at price. Think of the bearish strength compared to the bulls. Try and see how the bulls lost strength first before the bears started steadily taking over. See how this level compares with levels A and D.

I highly recommend placing a piece of paper over this chart and moving it bar by bar so that you can build your skills in evaluating S/R and T/R relationships. Remember to always start with the T/R positioning and evaluating turning point locations. Only then determine which S/R will be important given these positions. Remember also to only take positions largely with trend. If you have to take counter trend positions, take them only when the T/R position is to the right, that is, there's an almost equal representation between bulls and bears.

Let's look at a few more examples.

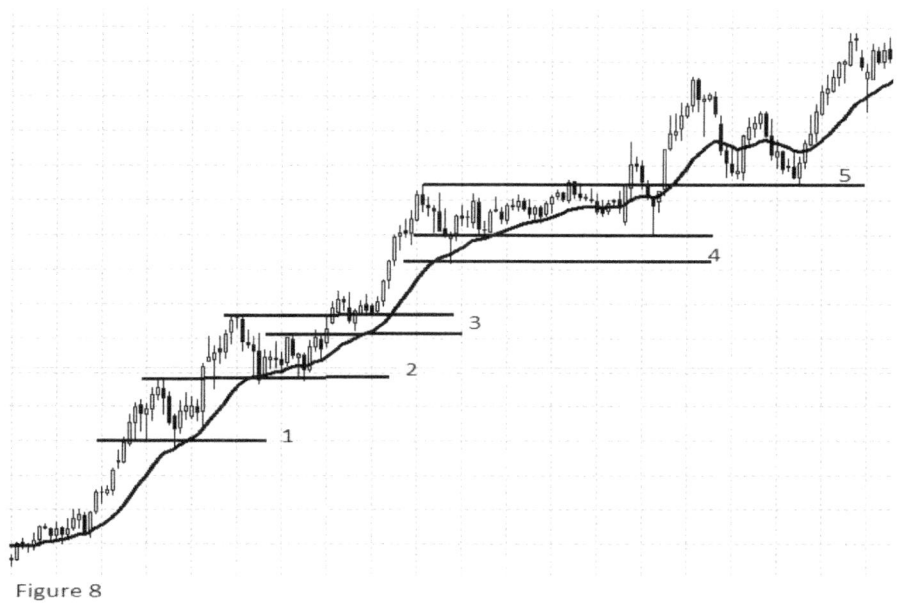

Figure 8

In figure 8, notice how as the trend progresses and as we move steadily from the left to the right of the T/R axis, price pulls in deeper into the trend and reacts only off levels which have some prior reaction. At 1, the bearish presence musters just 2 bars in its favor, one of them a pin bar slightly violates a previous pin bar. As price breaks past the previous swing high, that swing high immediately becomes a spot for price to react from on its way upwards. Notice that the S/R zones become progressively bigger as the trend continues. As always, cover this chart with a piece of paper an move it to the right.

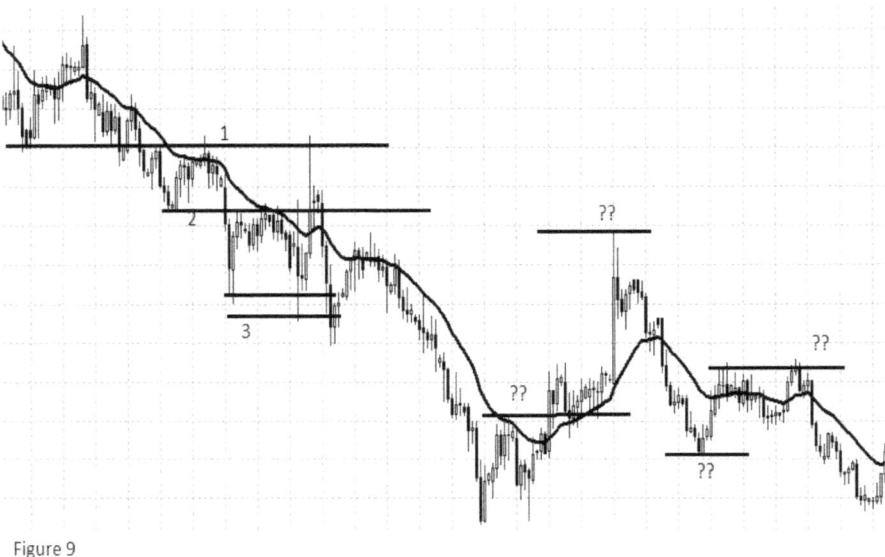

Figure 9

Figure 9 illustrates how chaotic the markets can be. Despite our best efforts at trying to decipher it, the market will always throw in nightmare fuel such as the chart above, which is close to impossible to trade real time. It starts off decently enough with S/R level 1 being respected. 2 is respected as well as we'd expect. It starts going pear shaped after that though. Price unexpectedly bounces all the way back to 1 and then slides down. Notice how despite producing 2 hits counter trend in a row, level 3 is pretty much irrelevant after price breaks past it.

It stops at a middle of the road level and then trend strength, which seems to be low this far, increases but in a half hearted way (notice how despite the lack of bulls, the bearish bars are small and until the end, the biggest bars are those with tails or wicks). Then follows what seems to be random price action with price stopping and reversing at levels marked by the "??" signs. This helps illustrate some very important points about the market. There is no method which will guarantee you a 100% win rate. So stop looking for it and understand instead what an edge means. Secondly, if you're unsure of the price environment, just stay out. There's no need to participate all the time. The market will always be there tomorrow. If it isn't, you'll probably have bigger things to worry about. So just sit out and learn to be OK with it.

Cover this chart with a piece of paper and progressively move it to the right. Try and understand why I've marked the '??' levels as such. In hindsight, they all seem to respect prior reaction levels but I've still marked them as such. Try to see why those prior levels which they're reacting to aren't the ones with the best odds of producing a reaction. Try and paper trade this chart and evaluate what your mental state is like and what you're asking and telling yourself about your abilities and this strategy. Chances are, they'll be negative. This can only be addressed by looking at your mindset which is beyond the scope of this particular book but is something which I will look at extensively in a later book in this series.

For now though, let us move on to the final piece of our puzzle. Timeframes and how they relate to S/R and trend decisions.

Chapter 4: Timeframe Mechanics

A lot of struggling traders tend to ignore timeframes and how they affect price action. More often than not such a trader is someone who day trades and sticks religiously to the 5 minute or 15 minute charts and takes only occasional notice of what is going on in the higher timeframes. What they fail to realize is that each timeframe is its own different world and that the timeframe directly above it needs to be taken into account when making decisions regarding trend and S/R. This goes beyond simply marking out important levels from the higher timeframe on the current one. The whole picture needs to be taken into account.

The first thing we need to evaluate when looking at a chart is the T/R position. The best way to do this is to adopt a top down approach to analysis. What I mean is start with the higher timeframe first and then evaluate your preferred trading timeframe. So if you prefer trading the 60 minute charts, evaluate the daily and 4 hour charts first. You will also need to look at the weekly but just to be aware. The frequency of how often you check the higher timeframe depends on how often that landscape changes. For example, a 15 minute chart warrants more looking at than a 4 hour chart. This approach holds if you wish to day trade or swing trade. Only those traders who position trade by taking positions on the weekly and above can avoid this simply because of the length of their holding times.

For the rest of us, we need to keep a very important principle of successful trading in mind. Our trades need to be in alignment with the higher timeframe as much as possible. When I say alignment, I'm not talking about trading with the higher timeframe trend or a specific S/R level although those would be examples of it. I'm talking about looking at the bigger picture which is painted by the combination of T/R and S/R. For example, if we have a situation on the 30 minute chart where the T/R is near the extreme right and we're approaching a good S/R level from where we can enter a counter trend position. Should we enter? Well, then answer depends on the higher timeframe. If the 60 minute chart is also showing a T/R near the right extreme and if the S/R level is present there as well, it makes sense to initiate a counter trend position. If, however, the T/R is somewhere near the middle and if the S/R is not as strong, it doesn't make sense to go counter trend since the higher timeframe isn't fully aligned with our timeframe.

This leads me to another important point which is: every chart is unique. You must resist thinking of trading in some formulaic way. Reading my previous example you might have been tempted to think of other combinations, like a strong S/R but middle T/R position etc, and ask what to do in those situations. This is an incorrect approach since every chart is different and it is impossible to make a judgment without looking at a chart. Furthermore, every trader has their own risk profile and you could very well have two traders looking at the same chart but come away with different conclusions. Neither of them need be wrong or right. You're only wrong when you start to prioritize someone else's view of the markets over your own judgment.

The best thing to do is to remember some principles as a broad framework within which to operate. This will give you freedom to manoeuvre while keeping you on the right side of the markets. Briefly the principles are listed below:

- Always trade in line with the higher timeframe picture. This means trading in line with what picture the T/R and S/R present.

- Trade as much as possible with the higher timeframe trend. Only trade counter to it when the T/R and S/R picture support doing so.

- S/R levels which are present on both timeframes (lower and higher) are stronger than ones present only in the lower timeframe.

- If the picture on the lower timeframe is unclear, either stay out or trade the higher timeframe until one does make sense.

Let's take a look at each point briefly. I've already spoken about trading in line with the higher timeframe picture previously in this chapter. The reason we want to do so is because the higher timeframe will assert itself over the lower one in the long run. Long run here is, of course, relative. The point is going against the higher timeframe is much like trading a weak counter trend pullback into a strong trend. The market will not move much in the counter trend direction and neither will it move for very long. Its just easier to take the line of least resistance and align ourselves with the dominant order flow. The same applies when it comes to timeframes. Once again, I want to stress I'm talking about the full T/R and S/R picture, not just the direction of trend or specific levels. You will always find the picture painted on one timeframe to be completely opposite on the higher timeframe. This is perfectly ok and you should not expect them to agree all the time. In such situations the thing to do is to ask yourself if the T/R positions on the two timeframes are similar and do they warrant a countertrend trade, that is, taking a position on the lower TF (timeframe) against the higher TF. If the T/R does not justify it, then stay out and wait for the pictures to align. This is just an example of course, as the overall picture is affected by the S/R as well. Refer to the charts at the end of this chapter to understand this better.

The second point, to trade with the higher timeframe trend, is really a subset of the first. I'm mentioning the trend specifically to highlight an important point which most traders might miss. Even if you do open a position that is with the lower timeframe trend, if it happens to be against the higher timeframe trend, you are trading counter trend. This has significant consequences for our risk management which will be explored in a later book. For now, it is important you understand and internalize this. Please note a significant difference between the first two points. I've mentioned to **always** trade with the higher TF picture but to trade **as much as possible** with the higher TF trend. For those of you confused by this, you must remember that trend and the overall picture are two different things. The overall picture is determined by the T/R (of which trend is a part of) and S/R. So it is ok to trade counter trend but only when the overall picture supports doing so. This is important to remember since you will very rarely find timeframes in agreement with one another, trend wise, while trading.

The next point is to do with S/R and its presence across timeframes. The more timeframes a level is present on, the stronger it is. Indeed, if a level is present as a strong one on multiple higher timeframes and is also strong on the current level, it will override any T/R considerations as explained in the chapter on support and resistance. Such levels should be considered automatic entries in the direction of the reaction produced. For example, in a bull trend across all TFs, if a support level has been hit multiple times an is present on 2 higher TFs than the one we're on, when price approaches it, irrespective of how strongly it does so, you must enter long automatically. Would we enter in a bear trend? The answer to this question is difficult to give without seeing a chart. The bull trend example puts us in line with the overall trend. For a counter trend decision to be made we would have to look at the T/R picture and will probably need an S/R level of high strength. Once again, remember each chart is different and do not try to transpose situations from one to another blindly in a formulaic way.

The final point has more to do with our mental and psychological makeup. This will be addressed in later books but briefly speaking, resist the urge to over trade or feel that you need to take part in every single market session. You might think that the professionals take part in multiple positions all the time on lower time frames and therefore to be one you ought to do the same. Nothing is farther from the truth. What someone else does in the market is none of your business. You have your own journey to complete and focus on doing just that. From a technical perspective, when confronted with a situation you do not understand, go up a timeframe until you find a level you are comfortable with. If there is no such level, then sit out. The same principle applies even when evaluating the T/R positioning. If, for example, you're unable to decide which level is a good turning point for the existing trend, then go up a level and designate that level's turning point as the appropriate one.

This brings up an important point in that, yes, different time frames will usually have different turning points. This is because the picture is different on all time frames. So you could have a scenario where the lower TF trend has reversed but the higher TF trend is still in the original direction. You must understand that there is no contradiction here. This is a very normal occurrence and you must get comfortable dealing with it. Simply build the overall picture and see what you get. If its unclear, simply stay out or go up a level.

I appreciate that this will be confusing at first. What you will need to do is practice extensively on your own charts and build up your skill levels in each of the individual components: T/R, turning points and S/R. Once you do this, I guarantee you will be miles ahead of your competition and certainly far better off than a trader who uses a host of indicators to make an entry decision.

The charts on the next few pages illustrate the thinking process.

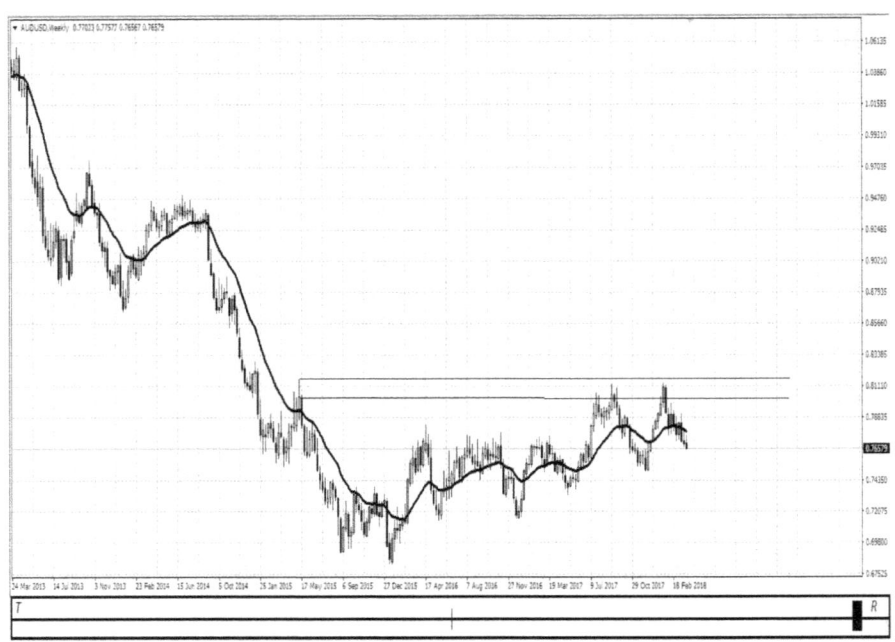

Here we have a weekly chart of the AUDUSD. As we can see price is below the turning point of the bear trend (marked by the 2 horizontal S/R lines) and is largely sideways despite the upwards tilt. So the T/R lies firmly on the right side. Let's now look at the daily.

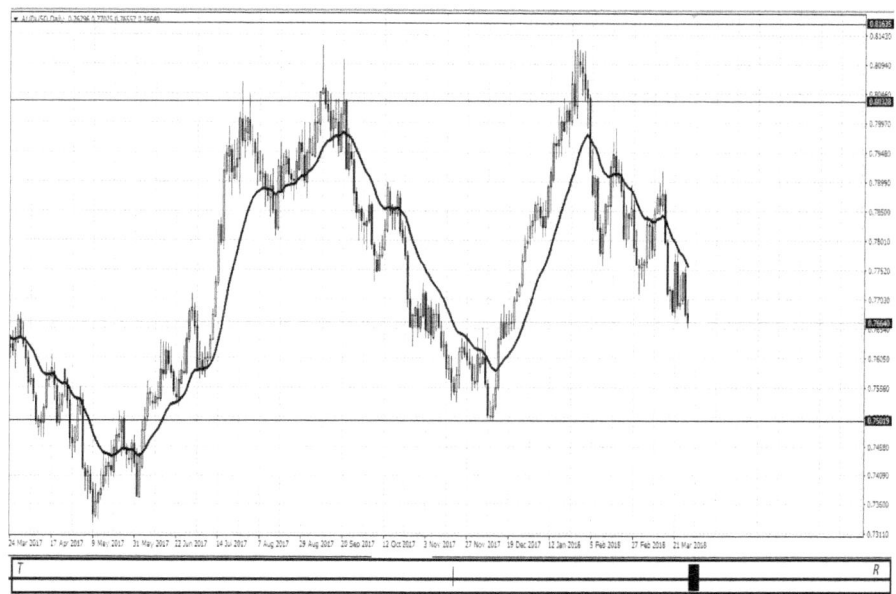

We can see on top the weekly resistance and near the 0.75019 level, the support on this time frame. This is also the turning point for the current bull trend on the daily time frame since it is the only point where the bulls have managed to overcome a strong bearish reaction. It might be difficult for you to treat a trend that will advance all the way down to this level as bullish but until this level breaks it will be so. Thus far we have seen that both the weekly and daily are low trend strength environments with both of them sitting to the right of the T/R axis. We note that the weekly is of lower strength than the daily. Let's drill down further.

Here we have the H4 chart. Here we see the trend is bearish but there is significant bullish involvement. The turning point is the first horizontal zone marked when looking top to bottom. The net horizontal zone marked is the closest swing point. The next zone marked is one which price has recently broken and is marked with dashed lines. I've highlighted this zone to illustrate how to think about which S/R level are key when evaluated on the basis of trend strength. The bullish involvement is clearly decreasing as we can see the extent of bullish pushback into the trend is decreasing. The previous swing down elicited a bullish response which went past a swing high. This time around though there was literally just one strong bullish bar before price went sideways and plunged downwards to break the previous swing low. This broken swing low is an S/R level. How do we decide if its a key level or not though? Simple, we look at the T/R position of this chart. T/R indicates this chart is in the latter half of the right hand side of the axis. This means we can expect decent bullish pushback despite the decreasing bullish involvement. Therefore despite this broken support level having multiple hits on the top of it, we conclude it will not function as decent resistance to stop the highly probable bullish reaction. We will instead wait at the higher swing high. You will also note: we're bearish on the H4 but bullish on the daily. So a short position here is counter trend. Well, remember the checklist. We take trades **mostly** with trend but **entirely** in line with the higher TF picture.

The daily chart has even more bearish presence than the H4 and is of weaker trend strength consequentially, despite being bullish. Therefore, taking a counter trend trade on the H4 is in line since we can expect the support of the bearish players from the higher time frame. If the daily picture were of higher trend strength than the H4, then we ought not to consider a short position on the H4 since we do not have the support or backing of the higher TF. This is how you mus reason your counter trend entries. Speaking of entries, we do not wait for some pattern to form or indicator to give us a green signal. We simply place our order at the level and place our stops beyond it and let the market come to us. This is how professionals trade and do not let anyone else tell you otherwise. I'll cover this topic in my later book on mindset and risk management but for now, you need to get comfortable with this way of thinking. Understand that waiting for some pattern is putting a barrier between yourself and the order flow which is the purest form of price action. Let's dig further now to the H1.

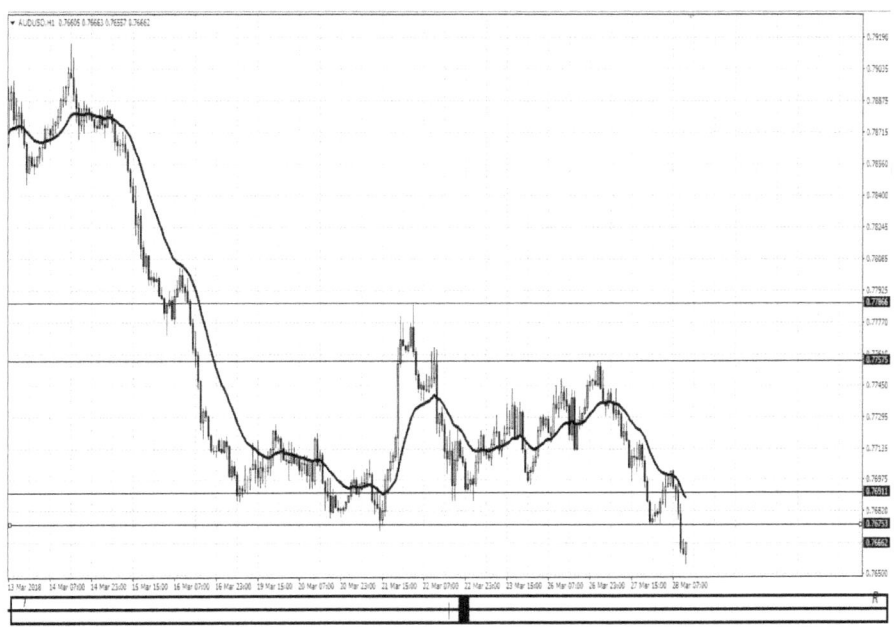

The H1 shows an even stronger bear trend as indicated by the T/R axis. I've marked it stronger due to the very small bullish involvement in the down leg which broke the support level. Remember, we value recent price action on the right side the most while progressively decreasing the weight as we look to the left. This chart poses an interesting question. A level which was deemed unworthy of our attention looks quite good on this landscape, at the very least, worth a second glance. This is because the T/R impels us to look at it. A short position from the recently broken level, **on this time frame,** looks a decent bet. It is with the higher time frame trend and the level has multiple hits on the other side of it. T/R indicates decreasing bullish involvement. The question is: is it in line with the overall picture of the higher time frame?

The answer is that it largely is but not definitively so. The higher TF has greater bullish presence so bearish support is not as forthcoming but it is in line with the overall trend and bullish presence is decreasing on both time frames. Does this mean we discard this opportunity? Absolutely not. We need to recognize that in terms of odds, this isn't as much of a slam dunk as it could be. The thing to do in such trades is to manage risk well. What this means is we need to recognize that the greater bullish presence in the higher TF will assert itself. Therefore, our position needs to be held for a shorter time and a larger reward than when we have the full support of the higher TF. So this means we enter from deep in the zone and take a closer profit target, in terms of pips, but in terms of risk reward, we are actually targeting a higher multiple. This is how you think about risk management and play the odds. I'll expand more on this in my book on risk management. For now, understand that we do not discard trade opportunities simply because they are not ideal. We instead mitigate their risk by adjusting our stop distance and entry points and target higher percentage rewards to compensate us for the risk we're undertaking. This ensure that in the long run, the math works in our favor.

Thus far we've seen all sorts of combinations of though process and trends and risk assessment. Well let's not stop now! Let's dig deeper and look at the 30 minute or M30 chart.

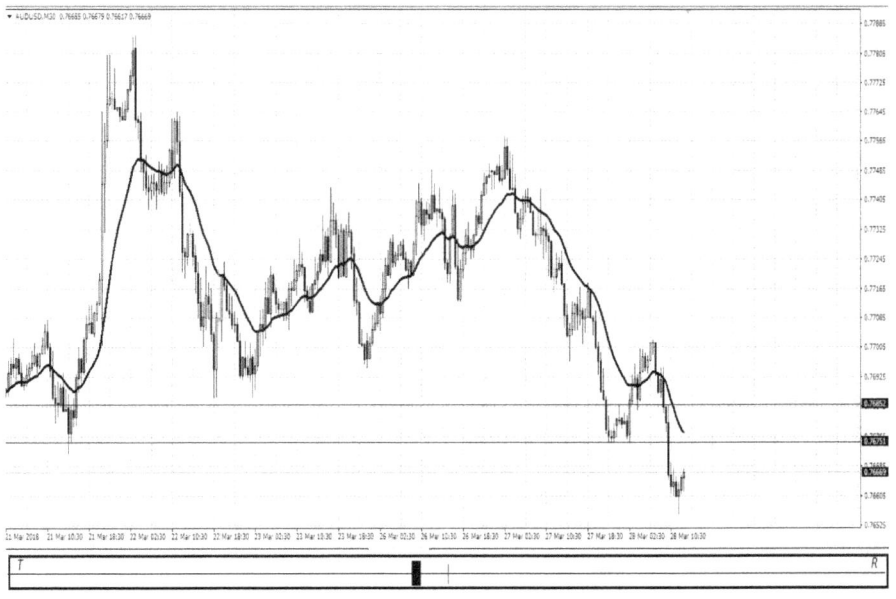

The M30 on the surface paints the same picture as the H1 chart. However, there is one crucial difference. On the final leg down we can see that the bullish presence seems to be increasing, as opposed to decreasing on the H1. If we were to imagine the T/R notch as a slider, on the M30, it would be moving to the right while on the H1, it would be moving to its left. Also note: the S/R level I've marked doesn't have the same width as the one marked on the H1, even though it is the same zone. This is because we only assess what we can see and every time frame is its own unique environment. We can however, conclude that this level, on this time frame is a strong one since it is present in a strong manner even on the higher TF. Therefore any pullback into this level would warrant a short. Due to the increasing bullish presence though, we would be better off approaching it just like we did in the H1 scenario: with a short holding time and a larger reward multiple. This can be accomplished with an entry deep in the zone as previously detailed.

You will notice, I've been using live charts to demonstrate the thought process. I haven't hidden any dates or instrument data so you can always go back and check on how this worked out. Understand something though: I'm not claiming that a short at this level will definitively work out. This is a wrong line of thinking. What I'm saying is that the odds are in my favor if a short position is approached in this manner. I'm also aware of my backup plan on every time frame if my position fails. Trading success is not determined by whether one trade fails or succeeds. It is determined by a large number of trades whose risk has been managed excellently thereby putting the odds in your favor in the long run. Thinking this way, one win or one loss doesn't really register. If you find yourself getting upset (or euphoric) with a few wins or losses, it is a huge sign that your mindset is not aligned with the principles of successful trading and that you need to teach yourself how to think. It is an unnatural way of thinking but it can be learned. It needs a lot of hard work and patience. Most of all it needs a huge amount of awareness and the ability to put your ego aside and admit you do not know everything.

Take your time with this chapter since it is very dense, like this whole book and series. There is a lot of information presented here which takes time to assimilate. You will find that as you practice on your own, you'll come back to this chapter and unearth more nuggets of information. Pay special attention to how the fact that different time frames are their own little worlds but that we're always aware of what's going on above that world and how it relates to the current picture. Also pay attention to how S/R levels are evaluated and how, depending on the T/R, the same level can go from non existent to extremely strong. There is no confusion here when you realize that each time frame is a different chart with different traders with different motivations.

This concludes our look at the basic principles. All that's left now is for us to tie it all together.

Chapter 5: The Complete System- A Live Trade

Thus far we've looked at the various elements that make up the basics of this method. We've looked at the T/R axis and how it interacts with the S/R and how, together, these two elements help formulate a picture of the price action on a given time frame. We then added another layer on top of it, that is, time frame congruence, which enables us to paint a 3D picture of the price action and increases our odds of success.

In this chapter, I will be walking through price action on multiple time frames and trading the charts using this method. Please note, these charts were live when I looked at them and the data presented in this chapter was collected over a long time period. My advice to you is to cover the charts with a piece of paper and move the paper progressively to the right and read the text along with it. Once you've done this, take some time to let the ideas presented here sink in and make a note of any questions or doubts you might have. Refer to the appropriate chapter to have these questions addressed. Once this is done, revisit the charts here and try to trade them yourself. I'm fully disclosing the dates and the instruments I'm trading so you can always download a charting software like MT4 or MT5 from any broker and look at the charts yourself. The charts I'm presenting to you are from the MT4 platform.

Due to the fact that most of you will be trading different hours of the market, I've chose to illustrate this method using the 4 hour and daily charts, sometimes even the weekly. This way, the price action will be applicable to everyone no matter which time zone they live in. Please note though that this method can be used on any time frame since the basics of price action and order flow remain the same irrespective of the time interval. We being first with the GBPJPY at the close of the daily bar on 8/31/17.

The chart below shows the position of the weekly time frame.

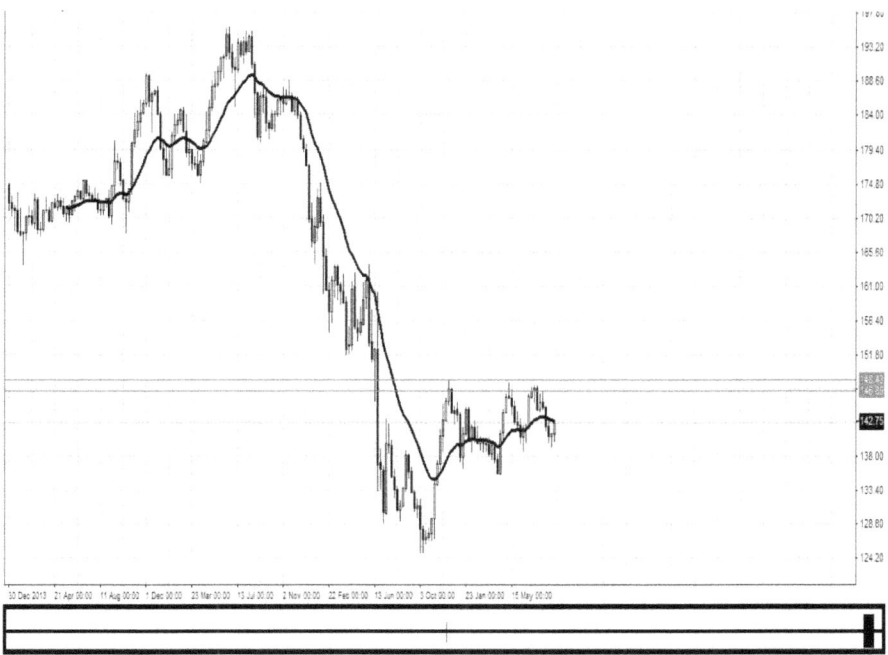

Price has been in a downtrend for a long while and is now consolidating within a range. The top of the range is quite clear whereas the bottom isn't. Hence our T/R position is to the extreme right indicating a range.

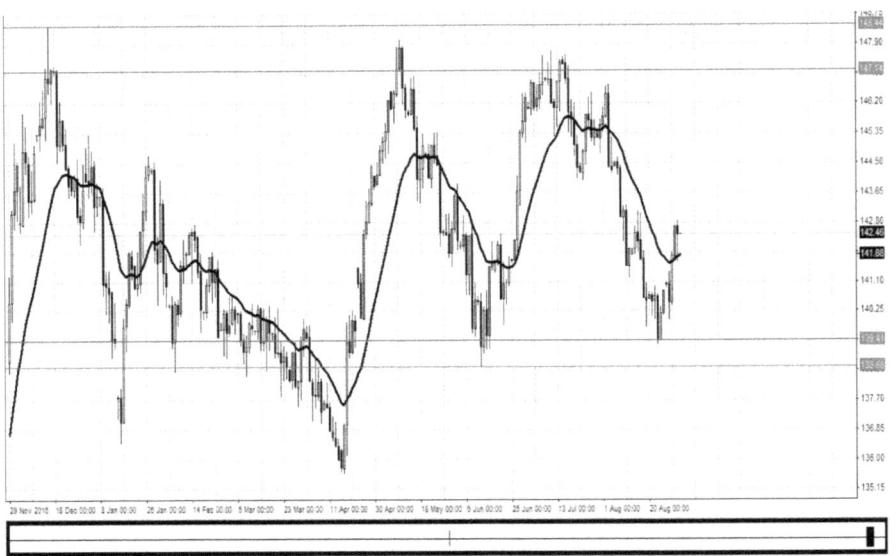

The daily chart shows price moving sideways. On top we can see the weekly resistance level. The daily chart also shows a support zone which is quite well respected on this time frame. We make a mental note that if price comes back to this level, we might have a decent long play off of this level.

The T/R position is to the extreme right once again due to the non directional nature of the price action.

The next page details the H4 chart.

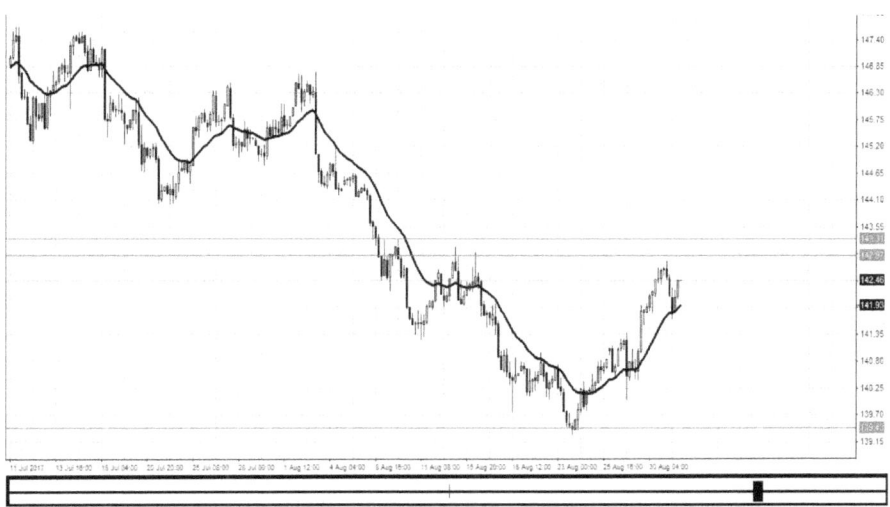

The H4 chart shows a downtrend which has started attracting a lot of bullish attention. While price isn't explicitly in a range on this time frame, we can see the buying activity is almost equal to the selling pressure. At the bottom, we can see price bouncing off the daily support level and headed towards the turning point on the H4 time frame.

Now that we've looked at all 3 time frames, let's recap. We have extremely low trend strength on the D1 and W1 (weekly) with the H4 showing greater strength relatively speaking. Price is approaching the H4 turning point. While this is a key level on the H4, we must keep in mind it is a pretty minor level on the D1 and as such, any short taken here is risky due to the lack of full contextual support from the higher time frame. After all, the level isn't present in a major way on the HTF (higher time frame) and the HTF's trend strength is weaker than the H4. Nonetheless, there is an opportunity here for a short term play. Since the HTF is sideways and the H4 is bearish, a short trade does have some merit to it. Therefore we place a short limit order at the level with a profit target of 3R (which is greater than the usual target of 2.15R). The chart below shows the trade location.

Please note: I'm assuming a fixed profit target for the sake of this walk through. Ideally, you should be able to read price action in real time and decide on the most opportune time to exit but this is a skill that needs building up to. Do not, however, make the mistake of assuming that those who take fixed profit targets are somehow inferior to those who do not. At the end of the day it is all about making the math work in your favor. In this case, since I've deemed this trade riskier than usual due to the lack of HTF support (contextual that is), I've taken a larger profit target because I need to be compensated for the extra risk. Also, I've chosen a 3R target for such trades and a 2.15R target for trades with lesser risk because this is what my statistics indicate will make me money in the long run.

The above is a very brief look at the risk management process which you absolutely must master if you want to have any hopes of trading successfully. The topic will be addressed in later books in this series but for now keep in mind the importance of this aspect of trading and simply remember that the riskier your trades are, the greater compensation or profit they need to make for your strategy to be viable.

The chart above shows price hitting our limit level and eventually hitting our profit target. We pocket a nice 3R profit before commissions for this trade. The trade had to be held over the weekend as you can see. I decided to do so because the risk parameters were fulfilled. These criteria will be covered extensively in the risk management book in this series.

The daily chart currently looks like so post this trade:

Price continues to progress within the range on the H4 time frame. After a week, we see price open early on Monday

(09/10/17) righto n the level. Price has actually gapped into it. Using the same deductive process as for the previous trade, we place a limit order, which is shown in the chart above, and wait for the market to hit our level. Price hits it as early as the very next bar (not shown).

Now all we need to do is to monitor this trade. Since the overall picture hasn't changed much, I haven't shown the weekly or the daily charts. When trading though it always pays to check the HTF just in case. In this instance even a cursory glance would confirm the picture hasn't changed so there isn't much to be added by showing those charts. The bullish pressure this time though is extremely strong and within a few bars, our trade hits its stop loss level leading to a -1R loss. The trade exit is shown in the next chart.

Since price has closed above the turning point, we must switch our bias to bullish on this time frame. Remember though the daily is still range bound and any long trades we take will not have great contextual support from the HTF. The daily chart below hows the current state of things on that level.

Price continues its bullish run and eventually arrives at the resistance level previously shown on the weekly and daily charts. Now, recall that the weekly and daily charts depicted a range after a bearish trend. The range top was very well defined so as price approaches this level we automatically place a limit short order at the level and wait for the market to fill us. The charts below show the order levels on the weekly (zoomed in) and D1 time frames respectively.

Our order is soon filled but again, the bullish forces are extremely strong and price hits our stop loss level shortly. The bullish force can be seen quite clearly on the H4 chart below.

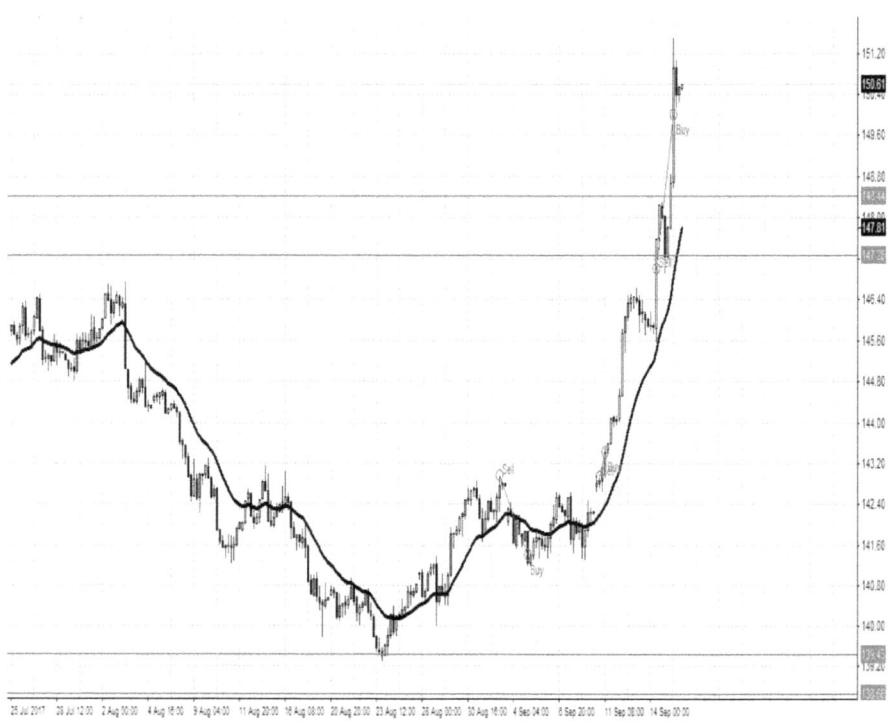

The size of the bullish bars has been increasing exponentially and the bearish participation is almost negligible. Given how easily price blew past an important level, we need to take stock of our T/R and S/R states again. Meanwhile we accept our loss of -1R and move on. This is a good point for you to perform a general checkup of your current mental state. Are you disappointed with the previous loss? Are you now telling yourself that the author is clearly bullshitting his way through this method? Are you telling yourself that you ought to close this book and buy another, more "reliable" method? If you answered yes to any of those questions, then you need to fix your mindset and expectations regarding trading. Trading is about making the odds work in your favor via simple math. It isn't some sort of a test or quiz one encounters at school or college where you need to score a 100% to get an A. There are profitable strategies that are correct 20% of the time. And here's the kicker: As a professional trader I can attest to you, every single professional out there (including myself) would prefer the 20% system to any system that is correct 80/90 or 99% of the time (no system with a 100% rate exists). Mull over that before you proceed. Why do you think that is?

The weekly chart is shown below.

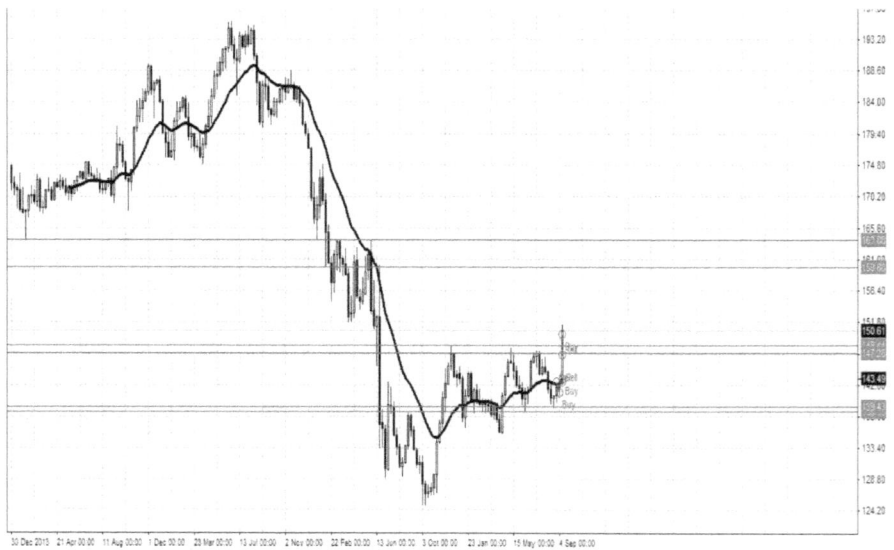

Price has broken out of a range and is looking bullish. However, it is still well below the turning point on this timeframe which is indicated by the zone above the current price level. The reason this is the most logical turning point is because of the extremely bearish reaction off this level. If price moves into this level, it would be an automatic short given how strong the reaction and thus, the level itself is. The T/R remains the same a previously,

Let us now look at the daily chart.

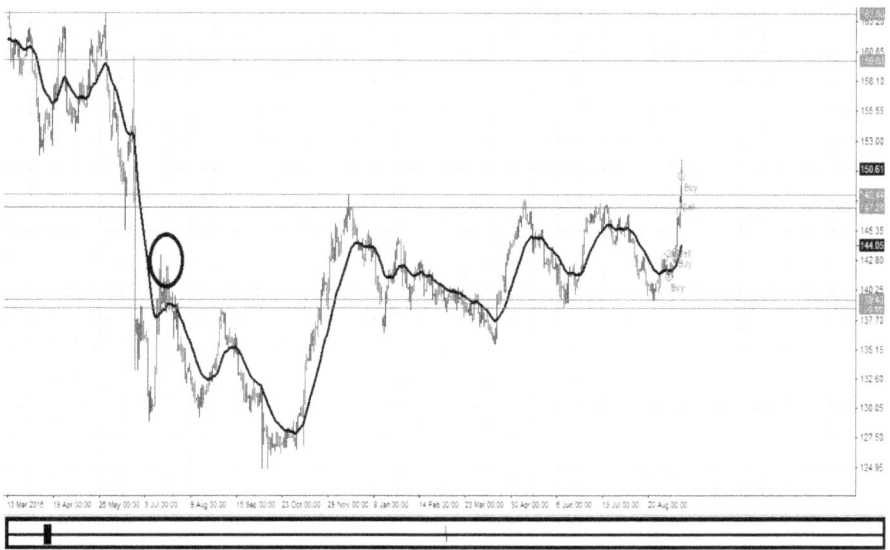

We need a zoomed out view here to see that the daily chart, while it was in a range that has now broken, had previously passed its turning point (indicated by the circle on the left). The weekly turning point is also shown lying above as resistance. Therefore we now have a situation where the daily is bullish, extremely so as indicated by the T/R, and the weekly is bearish with very low trend strength. Therefore, any pullback into the recently broken resistance will provide a good opportunity to go long on this time frame given the strong trend strength here and a weak, fully balanced situation in the HTF. My point is any long trade is unlikely to meet huge resistance to it from the bears since the HTF is showing a balanced distribution between bulls and bears.

Let us also look at the H4 for the sake of completing the picture. Given the bullishness on the D1, we might be able to get a more precise entry on the H4.

Here we see the broken resistance level and an extremely bullish trend with roughly equal strength as in the D1. I haven't marked the T/R on here since it should be obvious by now where the position ought to be. Having thus established our big picture, we move forward.

Price immediately starts moving within a very tight range on the H4. Given the size of the bearish bars and the short amount of time before the bulls are able to mount a comeback, we must conclude that this is merely a hiccup on the road of extreme bullishness. Given that the HTF is even more bullish looking, we need to enter this trend quickly before it runs away from us. Since the T/R is close to the extreme left, we do not need a very major level to enter this trend. The strong bullish presence will carry us through and a trade from the bottom of the small range formed should have extremely good odds of succeeding. Therefore we stick to our usual profit target of 2.15R.

The entry and stop levels are shown in the next chart. I've placed the stop below the 20 EMA as a precaution. If, for whatever reason, the minor level fails, the 20 EMA will act as a secondary dynamic support. It might be easy to think that since this trade has good odds, we need to squeeze it as much as possible and take a smaller stop and thus gain a larger reward multiple. This is precisely how traders goof up perfectly viable strategies through well intentioned, albeit misguided, thinking. Please note: We will shift our T/R a bit more to the right since the size of this small range is comparatively larger than prior ones occurring.

Our thinking is vindicated as price reacts off the level, fills our order and continues upwards eventually hitting our profit target. We bank a good 2.15R on this trade. Thus far, to recap, we've has 2 winners for a total of 5.15R and 2 losses for a total of -2R. Therefore, we're up 3.15R on our 4 trades thus far. (For those wondering R is the percent amount of your capital you're risking per trade).

The chart below shows the exit.

Price continues to move upwards but with clearly greater bearish participation. Our T/R steadily moves right on the H4 TF and the D1 TF with the D1 showing greater trend strength than the H4. A huge bearish bar beings price back to our previous level. As we can see from the chart below, this is a decent level but doesn't have great support on the HTF.

However, given that the HTF is exhibiting stronger trend strength we can justify a somewhat risky long off this level. As usual, we will need a bigger profit to justify taking this trade so we take a 3R profit target. The next chart shows the entry.

Price does bounce off this level and makes it close to our target but unfortunately dives and takes us out.

As we see from the above chart, price is making its way down to the previously broken resistance level. Now, on the D1 we are quite bullish with the T/R steadily moving right. The W1, though, is bearish with extremely low trend strength. We therefore set a limit buy entry order at the level in anticipation of it behaving as support. The reasoning for this was detailed a few pages back, please refer to it if you're unclear as to why this is a high probability trade. The chart below shows the entry and exit on the daily chart. Note how long we were in this trade and how price behaved before hitting our target. Place a piece of paper over this chart and move along with the trade. Examine your own thoughts and biases as you move along and your emotional range as you move steadily to the right. Based on everything you've read thus far, do you think you're reacting in a correct, probability based manner or in an incorrect, all or nothing, holy grail manner?

This trade nets us a good 2.15R once more.

From this point on, I would like you to move forward by yourself and reason out possible trade opportunities by using the though process I've detailed. I'm displaying all subsequent trades in the chart below on the H4 and D1 timeframes along with a table of the trades I've taken since the beginning. Move along the chart and make sure to keep referring to all the time frames. Please note that currently there is a long trade that is open and the S/R levels drawn reflect the current situation. Historically, you will have to draw your own S/R levels based on your T/R judgments.

H4 chart

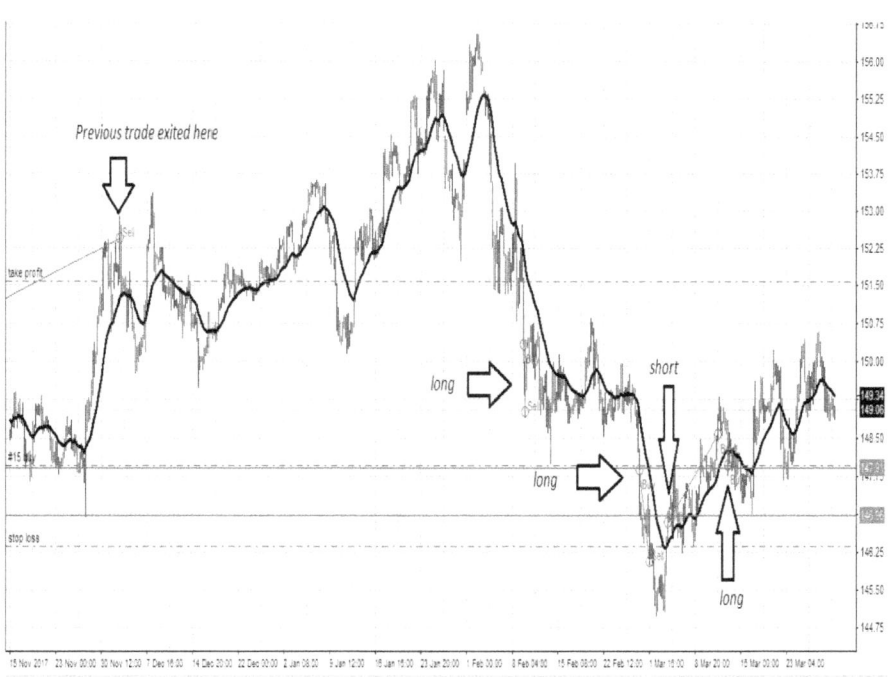

Next is the daily chart

The table below shows all the closed trades along with the execution prices. The far right column shows the number of pips won and lost. The column to its left is the overnight swap rate (this is explained in the previous book in this series)

Symbol	Type	Open time	Open price	Stop loss	Take profit	Close time	Close price	Swap	Pips
GBPJPY	sell	2017.09.01 15:12	142.96	143.48	141.41	2017.09.05 02:19	141.41	-8.72	155

GBPJPY	sell	2017.09.11 00:38	142.93	143.43	141.46	2017.09.11 10:51	143.43	0.00	-50
GBPJPY	sell	2017.09.14 11:16	146.99	150.00	140.27	2017.09.15 09:19	150.00	-2.91	-301
GBPJPY	buy	2017.09.19 13:18	150.28	149.49	152.13	2017.09.21 06:43	152.13	2.58	185
GBPJPY	buy	2017.09.25 15:56	150.23	149.63	151.86	2017.10.02 12:20	149.63	5.17	-60
GBPJPY	buy	2017.10.05 07:38	148.54	146.84	152.44	2017.12.04 12:30	152.44	43.30	390
GBPJPY	buy	2018.02.09 13:30	150.34	149.01	153.52	2018.02.09 18:44	149.01	0.00	-133
GBPJPY	buy	2018.02.28 12:37	147.85	146.05	152.04	2018.03.01 19:03	146.05	1.94	-180
GBPJPY	sell	2018.03.05 16:13	146.84	148.57	142.80	2018.03.13 08:00	148.57	-26.17	-173

Thus far we're left with 3 winners and 6 losses with one open trade currently in profit. This gives us a total profit of 1.3R over a period of 6 months with a success rate of 33%. While this isn't exceptional performance (admittedly it is below my usual profit rate), we need to keep certain things in mind.

We were trading just the higher time frames. By definition, the number of bars we're exposed to is lesser than on a lower time frame. The chart showing the daily time frame encompasses all the price action we've dealt with. As you can see, the number of bars is quite low despite us going over 6 months on the calendar. The next point to note is price was going sideways and such markets are notorious for producing lesser trade opportunities.

The final point I'd like to make is with regards to portfolio management, a subset of risk management. The entire topic is, as previously mentioned, beyond the scope of this book. You must remember though that long term profitable trading using just one instrument is impossible unless you trade the lower time frames extensively. The higher the time frame you trade, the greater the number of instruments you need to have in your portfolio. For the H4 and above time frames, I recommend having nothing less than 12 instruments. This way, your risk is distributed evenly and a below average performance on one instrument won't hamper your whole portfolio. Now, this single instrument gave us a result of 1.3R. Assuming our average R performance per instrument was half of this (.6R), our overall portfolio would have had a performance of 0.6*12= 7.2R. Assuming we were risking 1% per trade, this gives us a performance of 7.2% over 6 months or 1.2% per month on average with an open trade in profit. This is an annualized 15% in profit. If you risk greater than 1%, your overall performance increases automatically.

The above paragraph was to illustrate to you how performance is a function o things far greater than an entry decision. If you recall even our entry decision had aspects of risk management in it when we were deciding our stop loss and reward levels. You will appreciate how small a proportion the entry signal is of an entire trading system. Risk management is what decides your profit and loss ultimately. It is what your edge ultimately is.

Your edge is also a function of your mindset. Here's a rough statistic. Roughly 90% of you reading this book would have looked at an annualized performance figure of 15% and been disappointed. You would have thought you'd rather buy that guru's system which promises 200% per year. Here's a little thought exercise for you: Warren Buffett, acknowledged as the greatest investor of all time, has averaged a performance of

20% annually. If a forex system exists which can produce 200% or even 50% annually, wouldn't Buffett be better off investing his billions in the "guru's" FX system? Wouldn't he be a fool to sit in his Omaha office poring over financial statements and conducting research with his business partners?

A mindset which focuses on profits before risk is a mindset that will produce failure. I guarantee you that if you buy that 200% system, you will make money for perhaps a few weeks before donating your profits back to the market. This is because your mind doesn't yet know how to think about success correctly. You do not realize what a trading system actually is. This is why I felt the need to write a separate book on these two topics and frankly, even a book isn't enough. For now, go through the material here extensively and learn and practice this method until you know it backwards. This is a very discretionary method of trading and you will find that some times your conclusions will differ from mine.

Lastly, I'd like to point out, the record I've shown above is my actual live account which is why I haven't posted any dollar amounts. I haven't had the liberty of choosing a particular chart period where I could have shown performance of 10R plus. This is as real time as it gets on print. Before you buy your next book on trading, ask yourself whether the author has done this for you. If they haven't done this, ask yourself why this is so.

I hope you have gained a new perspective on the markets after this book. If you cannot make this method work for you, I apologize in case I haven't been clear. All I ask of you though is to give this a legitimate shot. I'm convinced you will be successful if you do.

Thank you for purchasing this book and I wish you the best of luck in your trading. Remember: you are a lot closer than you think you are. Always.

www.ingramcontent.com/pod-product-compliance
Lightning Source LLC
Chambersburg PA
CBHW070113230526
45472CB00004B/1237